The
BOOK
of
LIGHT

D1739046

The BOOKS of HEAVEN on EARTH

Volume Two

Written by Daniel Prok

The BOOK of LIGHT

More Books from Daniel Prok

Connect to God's Love, Light and Heaven

within Yourself through All of

"The BOOKS of HEAVEN on EARTH":

"The BOOK of LOVE"

"The BOOK of LIGHT"

"The BOOK of HEAVEN"

"The BOOK of LIFE"

"El LIBRO del AMOR"

Get them now as Paperback or eBooks online
and from book stores everywhere.

Get the audiobooks on Audible, iTunes and more.

For bulk purchase orders and to have Daniel speak to your
organization contact him through social media or
www.DanielProk.com.

Thank You!

Thank You!

Thank You...

In advance for sharing a positive review of this book with all
the people that you love, on Amazon.com, as well as on your
favorite social media platforms like Facebook, Instagram
and others.

Your voice matters in helping us promote a positive message
that will fill the hearts, minds and lives of all of God's People
with...

Love, Light and Heaven...

And create Heaven on Earth for the Collective.

The BOOK of LIGHT

The
BOOK
of
LIGHT

The BOOK of LIGHT

TABLE OF CONTENTS

The BOOK of LIGHT

Introduction

Another message from Jesus through Daniel

It is a great honor and privilege to share this message of Light with you.

While staying in Angel Valley near Sedona Arizona, I met a group of women on a retreat who seemed very familiar to me even though I had just met them.

One of them, who is now like a sister to me, mentioned that she heard of a book called "The Book of Love... by Jesus."

Since I love Jesus I said, "That sounds amazing! Where can I get that book?"

She said, "I heard the book got destroyed or removed from the Alexandria Library."

Intrigued, I asked, "So, have you read it?"

She said, "No."

Then I asked, "Do you know where I can get it?"

She answered, "No."

But after a few seconds she said, "But if you want it you'll find it."

At that point, I remember thinking to myself "Jesus...I want that book!"

The BOOK of LIGHT

The following morning, I was in my cabin preparing for the day and I heard a gentle voice in my mind say... "The Book of Love... by Jesus the Christ... Channeled by Daniel Prok... My Beloved... It is with great Love that I share these ideas with you..."

I had a sense that it was a message of great importance so I grabbed my microphone to record it. I closed my eyes, and took deep breaths to clear my mind, and as the words dropped into my mind I spoke the words out loud.

It was as though I was reading a speech that was written by Jesus.

And forty minutes later the initial message was complete.

I sat there for several minutes in what felt like a glowing ball of loving energy. My body and everything around me looked and felt radiant.

Then "Chapter 2" started to load into my mind.

So, I continued the process and "downloaded" the full audio of "The Book of Love".

A few weeks later, back in Sedona, the words of "The Book of Light" dropped into my mind in a similar way.

I spent the next few months putting both books in written form and publishing them so they can be shared with you.

Both books are messages from Jesus about the Love and Light of God that are inside of all of us.

II

The BOOK of LIGHT

They are not only inside of us... they ARE us!

"But how do we know that it's Jesus?", you may ask.

I know from the way the messages came into my mind, and then through my Heart and Soul. The warmth of the Loving energy of Jesus is beyond anything I have felt in my human form.

Also, the words of these books are so Divinely stated that it is beyond me to come up with something this magnificent!

As for you, you will have a knowing as you read the words. Feel them with your Heart and Soul. Feel them with the depths of your Being. You will know.

The Book of Light will uplift, empower and charge you to use the Light of God and the Love of God to make your life a masterpiece, and to help create a masterpiece for the collective here on Earth.

Thank you to Jesus for sharing this beautiful message so that everyone, everywhere can experience the Light of God and the Love of God in the way that he has.

God Bless you all with God's Light!

Daniel Prok

Forward

The use of this Book in Your Daily Life

A book of this nature is to be read, to be reflected on, to be shared, to be embodied... to learn and to express into your life.

There are so many of God's golden nuggets of wisdom, of truth, of knowing; and that will create a greater understanding of the Light of God within you, and the Love of God within everything.

Read this book before bed at night.

Leave a copy of this book by your nightstand.

Say the Decrees, and "Let there be Light", and other Declarations.

Speak those words over yourself and your family and all of your endeavors.

As you wake in the morning, read this book as a devotional.

Make similar Proclamations and Declarations from the Decrees, to declare God's promises over your life and all of your affairs in that day.

Programming your entire Being; your Body, Mind, Emotions, environment and all your activities.

Shining the Light of God through all of that,

Feeling the Love of God in all of that...

Being the Light of God and

Being the Love of God.

The BOOK of LIGHT

I AM God within You.

I AM God that is Always there for You.

I AM God who Loves you Dearly.

I AM God who had Tears of Joy at your Birth.

I AM God who Shines from within You.

I AM God who Gazes upon you Adoringly.

I AM God who is Always there for You.

I AM God whose Love for you continues to
Grow and Expand.

I AM God who will Always Provide for You.

I AM God who will Always
Protect you in the time of need.

I AM God that Saturates your
Entire Being with Light and Love.

I AM God the Almighty maker of Heaven on Earth.

I AM God within your Heart and Soul.

I AM God who Created your Divine Blueprint.

I AM God that is your Christ Consciousness.

I AM God that Gives you Everlasting Life.

I AM God that Blesses you with Immeasurable Favor.

I AM God that Loves You Forevermore.

I AM God that Smiles with Great Joy
as I look into your Eyes at All times.

I AM the God of this Universe.

I AM the Creator of All that is.

I AM God within You.

I AM God's Light within You.

I AM God's Love... Deep, Immense Love for You.

I AM that I AM.

The BOOK of LIGHT

As the Angels and Archangels sing in exultation, and praise and glorify the Creator of All that is, we shine the Light of God with great Love and intensity into your Heart, into your Mind, into your Body, into your entire Being, and create the Light and Love of God as your permanent state of being in your physical form.

Right there, where you are at...

right here and right now

in this present moment.

We Rejoice...

Hallelujahs and Hosannas in the Highest!

Peace,

Love and

Goodwill to all

Men and Women of Earth.

God's Love is Forevermore.

God's Light and Love Always Prevails.

God's Light and Love is Everlasting.

God's Light and Love Always Wins.

God's Light and Love is Now and Forever within You.

I Love you with all of my heart, and with all of the Love of the mighty I AM presence within me, the presence of God within me.

I say again, I Love You!

Your friend, best friend, loving guide, beloved teacher, caretaker, shepherd, and biggest fan of yours.

I have great admiration for you, and great Love for you as you go from a state of Consciousness based on discordant programming to a state of Consciousness that is your Divinity...

That is Fully Embodying God's Light within You.

Which is Fully Expressing God's Love within You.

God Bless You Now and Forever.

Jesus the Christ of Nazareth

Chapter One

An Introduction to the Light Inside of You

I AM the Light of the World...

As you also are the Light of the World.

All of the greatest aspects and characteristics of the Creator of All that is, of God the Almighty; all those properties, if you will, that I have fully embodied and maintain and expand within, all of those properties and characteristics are also available for you.

They are not only available for you...

They ARE You!

God's Light shines from the

Core of your Being before the creation

of the first cell of your physical body.

God's Light.

Radiant Light.

Loving Light.

Perfect Light.

All beamed from a source before the creation of your physical body.

This source of Light beamed so brightly and so powerfully, so perfectly, so purely, that this Light's expression combined with the immense Love of the Creator...

Combined to form the first cell of your physical body, and still today combines to form every cell of your physical body, every part of your mental body, every piece of your emotional body, every part of your Heart, every aspect of your Soul, every bit of your Consciousness, every one of the finest particles of what you consider to be your Being, every part of the life that you are living, every small speck of the energy that composes your society and reality that you live in...

Every part of that, every piece of that, every unit of measure within that, and even going deeper into every unit that cannot be measured, and the vast space between those units of measure...

All of that is the Light of God, all of that is God's Intelligence, God's radiantly beautiful, meticulously detailed planning for the creation of your life, the creation of this Earth that you live in, this Creation of all of Existence.

It is All God's Light.

Light so Pure that it Casts out All that is unlike it!

But as you have learned by reading the Book of Love, which goes into great detail about the Love of God within you and the Love of God which is what you ARE; in a similar way the Light of God within you, which IS you, which is always there for you, which is always making a path for you, Lighting the way for you... the Light of God that is always there in your Heart, in your Soul, in your physical body and in everything that you experience in life... that Light can be perceived as being absent, can be perceived as being distant, can be perceived as being pure darkness.

But those again are misperceptions of the Mind.

Your mind can, and has, come up with so many ways to look at the world that are not looking at the world in the way that God perceives the world.

Once again the mind gets caught up in the illusion, gets caught up in believing more in what it sees and hears than believing in what is right behind the illusion, and is right within the illusion, and is what creates the illusion.

The Light of God filters through your perception, your programmed perception of reality, the Light of God is shining brightly through that perception of reality.

You are literally projecting your reality from inside of your being through your mental body into the reality that you live in and experience.

5

And then looking at that reality, which is still just an illusion, looking at that reality and then perceiving something other than God's pure Light.

Looking at that reality and then perceiving chaos and darkness.

Looking at that reality and then perceiving lack, fear, anxiety, trauma and dramas.

The Light within you shines through your consciousness and projects the illusion of your experience which to you is your reality.

It projects the reality from within you into the environment around you.

And then, in response to viewing that projected reality, your mental body again perceives the reality that was projected from within you, and then comes up with more judgements, and conclusions about that image and that perception, which reinforces the perceived lack of Love and Light in this world you are experiencing.

But just know that the Light of God within you shines constantly, shines with everlasting beauty, shines gloriously, and is constantly amplified and magnified from the depths within you, and then shines into the world around you.

You are Light... as I AM God's Light.

When you live more in that Light. When you live more from the Core of your Being. When you live more from your Divinity, from your Heart, from your Soul, from your Spirit, which is all situated with God's pure Light...

When you live from that Light, and shine that Light through your Physical Body, through your Mind and into the world around you, that Light becomes all that is.

Living in the Light of God is such a beautiful gift and beautiful experience.

In my lifetime on Earth I learned to carry God's Light and Love as my permanent energy that I was emitting. I learned to live in the Light and the Love of God that was always within me, as that Light and Love of God is always in you.

When you live from that place, constantly beaming God's Light from the Core of your Godself throughout your entire being...

When you radiate God's Love from the Core of your Heart and Soul and throughout your entire experience and into the world that you live in...

When you do both those things, living as one with God's Light as you are God's Light...

Living as one with God's Love as you are God's Love...

When you do both those things, that life that you are living will become exactly the way that you want it to be, because you will be broadcasting such a pure signal.

You will be sending out God's perfect Light and Love from the Core of your Being into the world around you.

And from there you will transcend your programmed belief system; the programming you learned from the environment you grew up in, from the household you lived in, from your parents and siblings, from your extended family, from the schools you went to, from the friends you had, from the church or temple or synagogue or mosque, or any other part of your experience of your life...

You were Receiving Programming that

Created your Life as it is Today.

If you were to have been born in a country that is far away from the country that you live in now, and in that country they have different ways that society operates.

It is a different culture where they dress in a different way, they greet each other in a different way, they do business in a different way, they show affection to one another in a different way, they play different sports, they have different hobbies, they may have different religions, they have different beliefs and perceptions that they tend to have in their culture.

If you were to have been born in that foreign land, then you would have become a different person.

You would have become a person with very different beliefs, very different traditions, very different attitudes about yourself, and about society, and about the world.

If you were to have been born in this foreign land, and then grown to be an adult and then looked at yourself or someone like yourself as you are today, having grown up in the environment you grew up in, you would look at yourself and not even be able to recognize yourself.

Your hair would look different, your hair would be styled differently, the clothes that you would wear would be different, your posture would be different, the way you carry yourself would be different, the way you express yourself would be different, your tone of voice would be different... all this complexity of who we become based on the environments we are raised in...

Such a Complex System of Programming.

But when you can live in this new present moment and you can release all of the programs from within you that are based on limitation, that are based on lack, that are based on fear, that are based on disempowerment, that are based on unworthiness...

When you can live in the new present moment and fill that present moment with the Light of God that is always within you, and fill your mind with the Light of God which is always in you, and amplify the Light of God which is always in you...

And fill your Mind, and your Heart, and your Body with the Light of God, and amplify the Light of God... and amplify the Light of God even more.

To do that in this present moment and hold that vibration, that energy, that signal (especially in your mental body) you are clearing out the old energy patterns, you are doing a deep cleansing and reconditioning of your mental body...

Your Mind will be Cleansed and Purified.

Holding that Light... God's Light inside of You.

Maintaining that Radiant Vibrant Golden White Light.

Maintaining that within your Mental Body...

ESPECIALLY WITHIN
YOUR MENTAL BODY.

And when you do you are reconstructing your neural pathways in your Mind, your neural pathways in your brain. You are literally reconstructing your Mind to align with your Divinity, your Godself, your Christ Consciousness.

The Light that shines so bright and

created the first cell of your physical body.

You are creating a Mind that aligns with God,

that aligns with your Eternal Being.

The Eternal Glory of God that is within You.

And we continue to shine God's Light from deep within you throughout your physical form, transforming all discordant patterns, discordant thought processes, discordant belief systems, discordant perceptions, discordant behaviors, discordant attitudes, and routines, and processes.

As we shine that Light, which again is God's Light within you, as you are the Light of the world.

You are God's Light.

And as we continue to amplify that Light within you, your entire reality will transform into a reality of your preference.

A Reality that is Filled with Beautiful Things.

A Life that is Glorious and Wonderful.

A Life that is Happy and Loving.

A Life with Abundance and Prosperity.

A Life that is Healthy.

And a Life where you have Vibrant Energy.

A Life where you create Magnificent Things.

A Life where you openly Love others
and receive Love from others.

A Life where you Laugh, Enjoy and Serve.

A Life that is as God Created it to be
for You and for all Humanity.

That is a truly glorious life which has always been God's original plan for you to live in Paradise...

A literal Heaven right there on Earth.

The Kingdom of God is within.

The Light of God is within You.

The Love of God is within You.

And when the Light and Love of God are radiating from the Core of your Being through your entire Body, Mind, Heart, Soul, Spirit, Emotions, Feelings and into and through the entire reality that you experience, and continues to expand, and transmutes all the energies through the entire Universe...

When you live in that knowing that the Kingdom of God is within you, the Light of God is within you, and the Love of God is within you, then you will also live in the knowing that the Kingdom of God, being the Kingdom of Heaven, means that Heaven is within you...

And as Heaven is within you, and the Light of God is within you, and the Love of God is within you... as within so shall it be in the world around you.

The world that you experience around you is a reflection of the Light and Love of God that is shining from within you.

And when you continue to shine that Light and radiate that Love in both of their purest most beautiful forms, as you continue to do that as I have done that...

Fully Aligning with the

Light and the Love

of God within You...

As I AM the Light of the World...

I AM the Love of God within Me...

I AM Heaven on Earth...

I AM God's Pure Light.

14

Divine Decrees of Light

I AM the Light that Lights Every Path I walk on.

I AM the Light that Shines as Bright
as a Million Billion Trillion Suns.

I AM the Love from the
Hearts of the Angels and Archangels.

I AM the Light that Beams from the
Smile of a New Born Child.

I AM Light in its Purest Perfection.

I AM God's Light that Shines from the
Core of Every Human on Earth.

I AM God's Light that is
Everlasting and Ever Blasting.

I AM God's Light that Created
the First Cell of my Perfect Body.

The BOOK of LIGHT

I AM God's Light that Radiates from the
Hearts of God's Loving Children.

I AM the Light that Casts away all Darkness.

I AM the Light that Shines from the
Eyes of Jesus the Christ.

I AM the Light of the Angels and Archangels
in the Highest of the Heavens.

I AM the Light that Glorifies God
in Every Eternal Moment.

I AM the Light that Purifies all
Discordant Thoughts and Beliefs.

I AM the Light the Shines so Bright that it Shatters
the Shell that is Built around a Broken Heart.

I AM God's Light that Shines and Glows
with the Most Radiant Vibrations.

The BOOK of LIGHT

I AM the Light that Shined Eternally
from the Moment of Creation.

I AM God's Light that Glorifies the
Heavens and the Earth.

I AM God's Light that Beams Softly and Adoringly
on the Faces of all of God's Children.

I AM the Light that Dissolves any Impurities.

I AM the Light that Brightens my Path for Eternity.

I AM the Glory of God's Light within Me.

I AM God's Light Amplified to Infinity.

I AM God's Light Ever Expanding and Increasing.

I AM God's Light at the Core of my Being.

I AM God's Light in my Heart, Mind and Soul.

I AM God's Light that Radiates
through my Physical Body.

I AM God's Light that transmutes anything in my
Body that is not of Perfection.

I AM God's Light Shining Forevermore.

I AM God's Light with God's Greatest Splendor.

I AM the Light of the World.

I AM God's Light Forevermore.

I AM that I AM.

The BOOK of LIGHT

Blessings from Jesus

The Light of God is always there for you

as a permanent construct from the Core of your Being.

Live in this knowing.

Live with this as your permanent state of being.

Shining God's Light into the world with

everything that you do.

With every smile on your face.

With every look into another's eyes.

Shine God's Light.

Be one with God's Light.

Be God's Light,

as you are God's Light,

as I AM God's Light.

I AM forever at your service to guide you
into your full expression of your Divinity.

The full expression of your Godself.

Your full connection with God within you.

Your full and permanent connection
to the I AM within you.

As I AM Always with you.

And I AM Always there for you.

And I AM always loving you.

And I AM always shining the Light of God into your life.

The BOOK of LIGHT

Shining that Light from the
Core of your Being outward,
and shining that Light to Light the path
that you walk on each day.

I Love you Forevermore.

I Love you with all of God's Light.

I Love you with all of God's eternal Love and affections.

I Love you so much.

I truly Love you more than could
ever be expressed with words.

I Love Now and Forever.

Jesus the Christ of Nazareth

The BOOK of LIGHT

Chapter Two

The Infinite Light of God

It is with great Light that I share this message with you.

Light is what you would perceive as the energy of Creation. Light is information. Light is God's Divine planning. Light is within every last detail of the creation of your physical body, the creation of the Earth, the creation of your solar system, the creation of the galaxies, other planets and the Universe, and of all that is.

Light is that energetic frequency that you perceive with your human eyes. Photons of Light traveling at 186,000 miles per second. The speed of Light.

And as you understand Light, to your human mind, Light would have a limit, a limitation.

While Light as expressed by the Creator, when he used Light and used the power of his voice to speak that Light into Creation, with a burst and literal explosion of Light, the Universe was made manifest.

You are Made Manifest in a Similar Way.

A beam of God's perfect Light combines with the Love of the Creator, and with a burst of creation you are formed.

And from there you experience a rapid acceleration where the cells of your body multiply and split, and in due time the organs of your body are formed; your lungs, and heart, and eyes, your fingers and toes, all aspects of your physical body are created from the initial pulse or burst of Light which is God within you creating the physical body that you live in, and also creating everything that you experience everywhere you go in your physical world.

And while you experience life with your physical senses, you experience Light coming in through your eyes and being deciphered by your mental body.

To perceive things that you experience from the perspective of God's Light in you rather than from the perspective of your conditioned human mind and body... when you perceive things from the perspective of God's Light, as Light is within everything, then the reality that you live in, the wealth that you dwell in, this beautiful creation that you experience, shall become more and more like the original plan for your life from the Creator's perspective.

Again I will say...

God only Makes Perfect Things!

But if your human perspective or perception is that something is imperfect, then God has given you free will to believe in those perspectives and perceptions.

But from the perspective of God and from God's perfect Divine planning there are only perfect things that operate perfectly in this world.

Now you might ask...

"How are all things perfect in his world when things are

broken, have been destroyed, have crumbled?"

"How can you say that things are perfect when they look

like they are less than perfect?"

The perception of imperfection is a learned perception. It is a learned perception because humans tend to believe more in what they see, hear, touch, smell, taste... they believe more in what their physical senses show them than what is the truth.

All those misperceptions are learned from your environment.

If you were to have grown up in an environment of great wealth, luxury, and riches, and you grew up in a city of great luxury, wealth, and riches, then you would carry that in your knowing as the way that life works and the way that society is.

You would believe that you are wealthy, that you are rich, that you inherently deserve to experience wonderful and opulent things.

But if you were born into an environment that has been conditioned into a state of lack, a state of believing more in the material that you might have on hand and believing that that is your entire supply.

When God's Supply is Infinite and Everlasting...

And God's Supply in You is Infinite and Everlasting.

But if you were trained and conditioned to believe in those limitations and then carry a belief in your mental body that your world is not abundant then that is the experience that you have in life.

So the thing to note here once again is to say...

God only Makes Perfect Things!

God has made this Universe in a way that works perfectly. God has made your life in a way that works perfectly.

Every thought that you think is going out into creation, and begins to reflect that thought back.

So the thoughts that you think, and the way that you imagine your life to be, becomes your reality.

Also your beliefs work with perfection. The way that you believe the world to be is the way that it is for you.

Your emotions that you feel when you live in God's Love, and hold that as your permanent state of being...

That Love Becomes All that You Experience.

But if you have been conditioned to believe in less than that, and have patterns within you that restrict that river and ocean of Love, then YOU are the one who is cutting off the flow of that energy within you, and you are creating that reality.

All of this being done because no one taught you to believe more in the Love and the Light of God within you...

To believe more in the Love and Light of God in your Heart and Soul...

To live more from your Heart, from your Soul, from your Spirit.

If you were not taught to live in this way, then it is understandable that you would have picked up all the discordant behaviors, thought patterns, belief systems, emotional patterns, and ways of being that were modeled to you by the people, and society, and country, and world that you live in.

But now that you are reading these words, you are taking this knowing deep into the Core of your Being.

And now that you are resonating with that Light of God within you...

Now that you are resonating with the Love of God in your Heart...

Now that you are resonating with the Heavenly Host of the Angels and Archangels...

Of God the Father,

God the Son,

and God the Holy Spirit.

Now that you are resonating with all of these Divine aspects of the Creator of All that is, which are all within you.

When you live more from that space, that stillness, that Love, that Peace, that Light, that Prosperity, that Joy, that Well-Being within you... living more from that place of Eternal and Everlasting Wellness.

Now that you decide to maintain that as the state of being that you carry now and forevermore.

The BOOK of LIGHT

As God said,

"Let There Be Light",

and there was Infinite Light.

Infinite Light is Light Beyond Measure.

Infinite Light cannot be comprehended by the human mind.

The human mind likes to measure and quantify, as in the speed of Light, but God's infinite Light is infinitely faster than the Light that you comprehend.

God's infinite Light is infinitely expanding, infinitely increasing, infinitely radiating from the Core of your Being in every direction simultaneously.

That Light expands to the Core of your Being while simultaneously expanding, like a pulsing burst of the most vibrant, bright, shining, warm, glowing, radiant energy... expanding into infinity and eternity.

That is the Light within you,

that is the Light of God within you.

The BOOK of LIGHT

You are God's Light.

You are the Light of the World.

As I AM the Light of the World.

God's Light within me is the same God's Light that is within you, which is the same God's Light within the Hearts and Minds of everyone on Earth, which is the same Light of God in everything everywhere.

God Only Makes Perfect Things!

Live in that Perfection!

All that you have experienced that you perceive as being other than that has been conditioned into your mind from your experience.

But we are resetting your system to Be, Feel, Know and carry God's Light everywhere you go in everything you do.

Shining that Light from the Core of your Being through the world everywhere you go.

No matter what you are doing...

You are the Light of the World.

God's Light in You is the Light of the World.

I AM the Light of the World.

I AM that I AM.

The BOOK of LIGHT

Divine Decrees of Light

I AM the Light of the World.

I AM Light that Lights the Flame
in the Heart of Jesus Christ.

I AM God's Light that Created the
Heavens and the Earth.

I AM God's Eternal Light that
Blesses Societies Everywhere.

I AM God's Glorious Light made Manifest
in the Birth of a Newborn Baby.

I AM God's Purest Light
which transmutes all discordant Energies.

I AM God's Spectacular Radiance and Light
as in the Archangels' Wings.

I AM the Light which travels at Infinite Speeds.

The BOOK of LIGHT

I AM the Light that Radiates with Infinite Brightness.

I AM Light that Shines on the
Faces of all of God's Creations.

I AM God's Light in its Purest Perfection.

I AM God's Light that casts out all darkness.

I AM God's Light that Shines in the
Heavens and on Earth.

I AM God's Light that Shines from the
Depths of my Soul into All of Creation.

I AM God's Light Forever at the
Core of my Consciousness.

I AM God's Light that Radiates with God's Splendor.

The BOOK of LIGHT

I AM the Light of a Million Billion Galaxies.

I AM God's Light in its Eternal Radiant Perfection.

I AM God's Light in Every Cell of my Being.

I AM God's Light that
Transforms any negative Perspectives.

I AM God's Light that Creates
Heaven on Earth for the Collective.

I AM God's Light that Lights every dark corner.

I AM God's Light that Transmutes
Anything that is less than it.

I AM that I AM.

I AM that I AM.

The BOOK of LIGHT

Blessings from Jesus

I AM God's Light.

I AM the Light of God Within Me
and it is Eternally Self-sustained.

I AM is the Presence of God within You.

I AM is God's Light within You.

I AM is God's Love within You.

I AM is the Love that I have for you as Jesus the Christ.

I AM Forever One with God.

I AM Forever One with the Light of God.

And I AM Forever and Eternally

One with the Light of God within You,

as that Light of God is Eternal, is Everlasting,

and is Always increasing in its Radiant Perfection.

You are the Light of the World.

You are the Light of God.

God Loves You Eternally and Evermore.

As I Love You Eternally and Evermore.

Your guide, your Shepard, your helper, your loving hand when you need it, your big brother when you need me, your all powerful benevolent force in your life supporting you in the moment that you perceive it's not there.

I AM Always there with You.

I AM Always there Supporting You.

I AM Always there Blessing You.

I AM Always there Prospering You.

I AM Always there Shining the Light of God upon You.

And shining the Light of God

on Everything that you do,

Everything you Create,

Everything that you Perceive

with your Physical Senses,

Every Perception that you have

with your Mind.

I AM the Light and the Love of God in all of that.

Live in that knowing.

LIVE in that *Knowing.*

I Love You Now and Forever.

God's Light is you Now and Forever.

I Love You Forevermore.

Jesus the Christ of Nazareth

The BOOK of LIGHT

Chapter Three
God's Light is in Everything

God's Light is in Everything.

It is in everything that you see,

everything that you hear,

everything that you experience.

God's Light is at the Core of your Being;

is inside the physical structure of your Body.

God's Light is in your Mind.

God's Light is Everywhere.

And for you to live in that Light is your Divinity.

It is like a Lighthouse that shines its Light in a focused beam to help ships get to shore safely, and to help boats to stay away from dangerous rock formations.

41

It is time to use God's Light within you in a way similar to the way that a Lighthouse works, but also in a much greater way.

In a Lighthouse there is a Light source. The Light source sends Light in every direction, but within the Lighthouse are a series of lenses that reflect the Light in a way so that the Light beams with intensity in one direction to be that burst of Light that a ship needs to see in order to get the signal of its next best move.

So that Light in the Lighthouse, again that source of Light, can be harnessed in a way to do things to help, to do things to guide, to do things to be of service to humanity, to the world around you.

Using the Light within you to focus it in a way that helps the Earth, and societies on Earth, become greater than what they are right now.

Using that Light, that brilliant Light that does shine from the Core of your Being in every direction simultaneously; but focusing that Light through your mental body, by focusing that Light into Divine ideas that uplift society, to focus that Light through your eyes and your smile, to focus that Light through your voice, to shine that Light from your Heart and your Soul into the world around you, into your activities, into your experiences, into your family.

The BOOK of LIGHT

When you shine God's Light from within you

and focus it like that Lighthouse...

Focus it into the Child that you're Spending time with.

Focus it into the Group that you are Speaking with.

Focus it into your Business Plans that

are Making the World a Better Place.

When you shine that Light, and you are that Light, your life
and the world that you live in becomes more and more like
what God intended for the original plan on Earth for all of
God's children.

For You, and for All of God's People,

to live in a Gloriously Beautiful World that is truly

radiantly filled with Beauty and Magnificence.

God's Magnificence in Everything!

The BOOK of LIGHT

So shine your Light into your life.

Shine God's Light into the world around you.

God's Light when focused into that beam of God's Light...

Shine that Light through your Eyes
into the Eyes of a Stranger.

Shine that Light through your Smile
as you walk into a room that
you have never been in Before.

Be the Light of God in All Aspects of Yourself,
and be the Light of God in All things that You do.

That Focus of God's Light into Your Interactions.

Imagine a beam of Light; soft, warm, yet powerful and radiant... that Light shining so brightly from within you through your being, shining from your entire face, like that Lighthouse shining into the darkness, your Light shines so bright that it transmutes all darkness into Light.

God's Light is Eternally Abundant.

The Supply of Light Never Ends.

The supply of God's Light in the form of Divine ideas for you to implement and utilize to Bless your life, to Bless your family, to Bless your community, to Bless your church, to Bless your temple, to Bless your organization, to Bless your city, and country, and all of the Earth.

Using that infinite Light of God in the form of Divine ideas and plans to make your life, and all the layers of your experience of life... to send that glorious Light through All of Creation everywhere.

And while you can perceive the Light in you to be focused in that way, also know that that is just one way to utilize God's Light with focus.

The BOOK of LIGHT

Another way to utilize the

Infinite Light of God is to

BE that Light...

BE that Light!

And when you are that Light, you are more like the Light of a million billion trillion suns.

That is the Light of God within you, like the Light of a million billion trillion suns.

Hold that image, hold that knowing, hold that truth of the Light within you.

You are the Light of God

that Shines like a

Million Billion Trillion Suns!

That is your Original Blueprint.

That is the Christ Consciousness within you.

That is your Divinity.

That Light is at the Core of your Being.

The Light of God,

which shines brighter than a

Million Billion Trillion Suns...

That is God's Light within you!

And that Light is Eternal,

is Infinite and is Forevermore.

And from that *knowing* within you,

all that your old self would

have perceived as chaos,

or something to be afraid of,

or lack of health or

lack in any way,

shape or form...

All of that Disappears.

It never existed from the state of Consciousness,

which is your Permanent state of Consciousness,

of Oneness with the Creator of All that is,

of Oneness with God's Light.

The BOOK of LIGHT

"Let There Be Light" Decrees

Let there be Light in all of my Actions.

Let there be Light in all of my Transactions.

Let there be Light in all of my Thought Processes.

Let there be Light in all of my Perceptions.

Let there be Light in all of my Physical Senses.

Let there be Light in All Places
that I go and in Everything that I Do.

Let there be Light in all Public Offices.

Let there be Light in the Hearts and
Minds of the Leaders of every Country.

Let there be Light in my Financial Prosperity.

The BOOK of LIGHT

Let there be Light Forevermore in my Divinity.

Let there be Light in every aspect of my Being.

Let there be Light in all of God's Creation.

Let there be Light at the Core of Every Manifestation.

Let there be Light ever Expanding
through all Space and Time.

Let there be Light in all Societies on Earth.

Let there be Light in every Particle of God's Creation.

Let there be Light in the Space
between each Particle of God's Creation.

Let there be Light at the Core of my Knowing.

Let there be Light at the Core of my Being.

The BOOK of LIGHT

Let there be Light Saturating my
Subconscious Programming.

Let there Be Light and its
Eternal Glory of Manifestation.

Let there be Light within every Human Expression.

Let there be Light within the way I Perceive
Everything that I Experience.

Let there be Light that creates Eternal Sunshine.

Let there be Light that is God's
Eternal Glory in my Life.

Let there be Light that is God's Everlasting Goodness.

Let there be Light Transmuting
Everything at a lower Vibration.

The BOOK of LIGHT

Let there be Light as God's Purest Manifestation.

Let there be Light in the Hearts and Minds
of all People on Earth.

Let there be Light in all Sentient Beings.

Let there be Light Now and Forevermore.

Let there be Light in the Hearts and Souls
of Everyone on Earth.

Let there be Light in the Hearts and Souls
of Everyone Everywhere.

Let there be Light.

Let there be Infinite Light.

Let there be Everlasting Light.

Let there be Eternal Light.

Let there be Light as God has Always intended.

Let there be Infinite and Everlasting Light
Expressed in All of Creation Now and Forevermore.

I AM the Light of the World.

I AM God's Light within You.

I AM that I AM.

The BOOK of LIGHT

Blessings from Jesus

I Love and Bless you.

As you shine your Light into the world from the Core of your Divinity before you were created; bursting outward, and shining with such radiance that you transform your life and the collective experience.

God's Original Plan for Heaven on Earth and the Kingdom of Heaven to be that permanent construct within you, and within the world that you live in now and forevermore.

Your Light within You,

and the Expression of that Light within You,

is of Great Importance.

That Light within you is to be used to transform this world into that beautiful Paradise and Oasis, that literal Garden of Eden that God has always had in store for you.

There is no more time to live in a state of being that does not involve your full connection with your Heart, with your Soul, with your Divinity, and with God's Love and Light within you.

Right Now is the Moment to BE the Light.

Right Now is the Moment to BE the Love of God.

Right now is the moment to know this so deeply

that it changes the way that you operate.

It Changes the way You Carry Yourself.

It Changes the way You Speak to others.

It Changes the way you Smile.

It Changes the way You Communicate.

It Changes Your Life,

and Your Beautiful and Unique

Expression of Life into the

World around You.

You are both like the Lighthouse

Lighting the way for others,

as well as being God's Light

that Shines as Bright

as a Million Billion Trillion Suns.

Be both versions of that Light in the World.

Be the Light of God in the World.

You are the Light of the World...

as I AM the Light of the World.

As God's Light is the Light of All of Creation.

I Love you and Bless you Forevermore.

Jesus the Christ of Nazareth

The BOOK of LIGHT

Chapter Four

The Immensity of God's Light within You

And God said, "Let there be Light"

and there was Light everywhere. Genesis 1: 3.

When God spoke these words, "Let there be Light", in that moment there was Infinite Light everywhere and it has been self-sustained since that moment.

God's Light is so immense, when you try to think about it and comprehend it, it is beyond your capacity to do so, as far as your capacity of understanding within your human mental construct.

But when you live in your Divinity, when you live in your Soul, and your Spirit, you are able to get a greater perspective of the Light of God within you, and the Light of God within everything.

Similar to the concepts of Love from the teachings of "The Book of Love", "The Book of Light" is written to give you a greater grasp, a greater understanding, a greater knowing of the immensity of God's Light within you.

And that Light within you is the same Light that is in All of Creation.

Going from one level of Understanding,

and expanding your Consciousness to

an even greater level of Understanding,

and an even more broadly

expanded Perspective...

That Process of Expansion into

greater Understandings,

greater Knowings and

greater Perspectives

is Eternal.

As the Light of God is Eternal,

as the Love of God is Eternal;

your Perspectives,

Understandings,

and Knowings

of the Light and Love of God

will always go from

one level to another.

Your Life will Always go from One Level to Another.

There is Always another way to Experience God.

There is Always another way to Connect to God.

There is Always another way to Reinforce

Your Connection to God.

There is Always a way to Enhance

Your Oneness with God.

And as we continue on that path, and that journey within yourself to Oneness with God's Light, you will realize that the brightness of the Light, the Divine Intelligence, the Divine Thought, your Divinity, your Divine Blueprint, your Christ Consciousness... the Light within all of that, will continue to amplify to the Core of your Being.

And whatever you feel as the depths and the Core of that Being, and the Light that now reaches that core, there will be more.

More perfection,

more splendid brilliance in that Light,

more of the Light in you transforming

any darkness within your being

from your perspectives that

have caused there to be anything

but God's Light within you.

We are Going Deep and We are Going Wide.

Imagine that million billion trillion suns all simultaneously joining into one point of Light, and that Light of all those million billion trillion suns resting at the Core of Creation in the Core of YOU; pulsing, beating, as the heart of God beats within you.

Shining Brilliantly!

Resting deep within your Soul,

deep within your Heart,

deep within your Core.

That is God's Light that shines from within You.

That is God's Light that shined in order to create You.

The BOOK of LIGHT

God said, "Let there be Light"

and that Light is what created You.

That Light created this Earth you live in.

That Light created this world,

this solar system.

That Light created everything that

you've ever experienced,

or ever could experience...

That Light created *Everything!*

And we will continue to go deep within your Consciousness, to have God's Light like the million billion trillion suns, as it sits deep in your Consciousness, deep at the Core of your Being.

Imagine that Light starting to spin.

And as it spins, it sends Light in every direction. And it spins on one axis but then that axis starts to rotate.

So while that Light of God spins on its axis, that axis also spins and rotates in every direction at infinite speed.

Then that Light is shining and expanding and glowing everywhere, sending that throughout All of Creation, sending that throughout all aspects of your life.

That Light of God transforming everything from the Core of your Being throughout All of Creation, and to the farthest reaches of eternity, which has no measure...

That Light of God Continues to Shine.

Sit in that Energy for a Moment.

Know that as your Permanent state of Being.

The BOOK of LIGHT

Know that source of God's Light is your Light,

the Light that shines within you.

Know that Light,

Be that Light,

You are that Light...

as I AM that Light of God within you.

Carry that Light into Everything that you do,

Everywhere that you go.

That Knowing of that Oneness

with the Light of God within you,

then using that Knowing,

and that truth to transform the way

that you Perceive your world.

Perceive the World from the Perception of
Light Perceiving Light.

Perceive the World from the Perception of
Love Perceiving Love.

Perceive the World as
Beauty Perceiving Beauty.

Perceive the World as
God's Glory Perceiving God's Glory.

And as you practice perceiving life in this way...

Perceiving Life from a State of Light.

Perceiving Life from a Perspective of Love.

Perceiving Life from the Perspective of God's Glory.

Perceiving Life from the Perspective of
God's Beauty in Everything.

The BOOK of LIGHT

When your Perspectives change,

your Reality changes,

your Life changes.

Perceiving things the way God Perceives them.

Perceiving things from the Perspective of Love and Light.

That Divine Perspective,

and Divine Knowing,

and Divine state of Being

will help you live in and create

a Masterpiece of Your Life.

A Masterpiece in All of your Affairs.

A Masterpiece in All of your Relationships.

A Masterpiece in your Eternal Being.

You are God's Masterpiece.

You are God's Greatest Treasure.

You are Loved by God Beyond Measure.

The BOOK of LIGHT

And the Immensity of God's Light

within You is the Real You.

You are God's Light.

You are the Light of the World.

As I AM the Light of the World.

The BOOK of LIGHT

"Let There Be Light" Decrees

Let there be Light at the Core of my Being.

Let there be Light in all of Infinity.

Let there be Light Everlasting and Ever Blasting.

Let there be Light in all of my Relationships.

Let there be Light in all of my Friendships.

Let there be Light in all my Communications.

Let there be Light in all of Humanity's Relations.

Let there be Light flowing
from one Leader to another.

Let there be Light Shining from the
Heart of an expectant Mother.

The BOOK of LIGHT

Let there be Light in all Businesses on Earth.

Let there be Light in the use of all Technologies.

Let there be Light in the
formation of new Communities.

Let there be Light in the
Treaties made between Countries.

Let there be Light in the
Peace between warring Societies.

Let there be Light in all those
Powers that affect the People on Planet Earth.

Let there be Light within the
Minds of all Scientists and Engineers.

Let there be Light in all
Corporations and Governments.

Let there be Light in all Countries and Oligarchies.

The BOOK of LIGHT

Let there be Light in the
Peace Treaties that set all captives Free.

Let there be Light in the
Hearts and Minds of all Sentient Beings.

Let there be Light in its Highest of Vibrations.

Let there be Light in all of God's Eternal Creation.

Let there be Light to the Core of Mother Earth.

Let there be Light.

Let there be Light within the
Pulse of Everyone on Earth.

Let there be Light that Sparks the Flame
that ignites the Fire of God within All of Us.

Let there Be Light that Amplifies the
Sacred Heart Fire of God within Us.

The BOOK of LIGHT

Let there be Light Now and Forevermore.

Let there be Light to the Eternal Depths of my Core.

Let there be Light Everlasting and Ever Blasting
for all of Eternity.

Let there be Light Expanding into all of Infinity.

Let there be Light in the
Golden White Light of our Creator.

Let there be Light in all of God's Splendor.

Let there be Light with the
Singing of the Angels and Archangels.

Let there be Light from the
Heart of Jesus Christ to my Heart.

Let there be Light... Let there be Light.

Let there be Light.

The Gifting of Light from Jesus

I give you these as codes of Light, transmissions of Light, Light frequencies; to embed them into your Consciousness connecting you to the Core of your Divinity.

As these words have always existed and resonated to the Core of your Being; these Light codes, these Decrees, these Affirmations carry great power to transmute any energies that are unlike them.

Use these Divine Light codes, these Divine Decrees, these Divine Affirmations...

Proclaim, Declare and Decree

them over your Life and

into the World that you Experience!

Use these daily to reinforce your connection to this knowing.

Use these daily to reinforce this as your permanent state of being.

Use these daily to live in your Divinity.

Speak them with great Force and Power!

Again...

Proclaim, Declare, and Decree...

In the Name of Jesus the Christ!

In the Name of God the Father Almighty!

In the Name of the Holy Spirit!

In the Name of the Heavenly Host

of Angels and Archangels!

With all of that as the force, and strength, and power, and life within you, using all of that to Proclaim, Declare, and Decree these aspects of your Divinity into your life as you are experiencing it now.

Connecting you to your Godself, to your Higher self, to your Heart, to your Soul, to your Christ Consciousness, to God within you; connecting yourself to that which is actually reconnecting to what has always been there.

And from that place, programming your Mind, programming your Body, programming your Emotions, programming the world that you live in from that Divinity.

Going deep within and then transforming everything into God's Love, God's Light and transforming everything into the Highest Frequencies of the Heavens happening right here and right now, in the center of your Being, the center of your Consciousness, and the Core of your Soul.

You are God's Light.

You are God's Love.

You are God's Most Treasured Masterpiece.

You are God's Infinite Glory.

And you are the immensity of God's Light

within you Now and Forevermore.

Infinite Blessings.

Infinite Light.

Infinite Love.

Infinite Prosperity.

Infinite Happiness.

Infinite Beauty.

Infinite Wisdom.

Infinite Well-Being in your

Body, Mind, and Spirit.

May God's infinite, abundant treasures continue to reveal themselves in the way that you experience life from the inside of your Being, and the inside of your physical Body, and the Core of Yourself, and expand it into all aspects of your physical world that you live in.

It is with great joy that I share this Book of Light with you.

It is with great Joy that I share God's Light with you.

It is with great Joy that I share the
Immensity of God's Light with you.

And it is with great Joy that I will continue
to always be with you.

Amplifying the Light of God.

Improving the Light of God within You.

Expanding your awareness of the
Light of God within You.

The BOOK of LIGHT

I will Eternally be there to Shine that Light,

and to also Express that Love

to you in Infinite ways.

I Love You Forevermore.

I Love You Eternally.

And may the Immensity of God's Light

Shine within you Now and Forevermore.

I Love you Now and Forever.

Jesus the Christ of Nazareth

Chapter Five

God's Light in this World

As God's children, we are all bearers of God's Light.

It is in every aspect of who we are, although human perception may perceive otherwise.

But the Light within us is always there.

God's Light is always there.

And from this frame of reference, there is a knowing that there is Light within everything, and that you are a bearer of God's Light.

You literally shine so brightly that it would be like a person looking directly into the sun.

You Shine with the Light of the Creator of All that is.

The Light of God Shines from within You.

The BOOK of LIGHT

And as a bearer of God's Light, as someone who is one with God's Light, and as someone who has the awareness and is connecting to that knowing, that being of God's Light...

Connecting to that understanding, connecting to that knowing, connecting to that being...

Literally *being* God's Light.

You are God's Light in this World...

as I AM God's Light in this World.

You are the Light that Brightens

the room that you walk into.

You are the Light that Uplifts your Family

when your Loved ones are down.

You are the Light that Brings a Message of

Good Tidings and Great Joy to the World.

God's Light is YOU.

You are God's Light.

And the eternal nature of God's Light within the Core of your Divinity, your Christ Consciousness, your Divine Blueprint, that Light is there within your Core to shine, and to be the bright shining example of what God's Light looks like in human form.

And to combine the Light of God and the Love of God within your being, and radiating all of that out into the world around you... sending Love to those who need it.

Shining the Light of God from within you into the places that you go; everywhere you go, in every eternal moment, you are one with the Light of God, and the Love of God to the Core of your Being.

You are God's Masterpiece.

And as you shine God's Light in your unique ways that will be shown to you, the unique ways that are best for you to shine God's Light...

Like that Lighthouse that shines the Light through specific reflectors and prisms, your unique structure of your Divine Blueprint, the way that God made you unique and beautiful and glorious...

As you shine your Light from deep within you through your perfect expression of your True Natural Self, of your Godself...

As you express yourself in your own special way, and you shine the Light in you through your experience, through your actions, through your activities...

As you do this more and more you will also be an example to others; an example of God's Light and Love shining in the world, Loving the world, expressing yourself with your true Soul's expression in the world.

You will be an Example for others to Follow.

And as others are activated by God's Light within you, the Light within them will also amplify and expand.

And as the Light within them activates the Light within the people that they know, and that they encounter, there is a chain of events that happens as God's Love and Light is activated in the Hearts and Minds of each individual Consciousness.

The BOOK of LIGHT

So, from one person,

they Light the fire within many others,

and they Light the fire within entire Communities,

and those Communities send the

Light and the Love of God through

Cities, States, and Countries;

and those Cities, States, Countries, and Communities

send the Light of God and

send the Love of God

throughout All of the Earth,

All of the World,

and All of Creation.

Connecting with Your Divinity

is the First Thing to do.

Then, Sharing the Light of God

and the Love of God within You

with those around You,

is the Next Thing to Do.

And finding creative ways to share that Love and share that Light with the world in the way that is best for you is what God made you here to do.

You are the Light of the World.

You are God's Love in Human Form.

You are God's Masterpiece.

To help create the masterpiece that is already within the Hearts and Minds of the people that you know, and for all of humanity.

The Light of God, the Love of God, the masterpiece of God's Creation which is the masterpiece that God created when He created You.

Expressing that Masterpiece,

expressing that Masterpiece within you,

expressing that Masterpiece...

The BOOK of LIGHT

God's Glorious Magnificent Masterpiece,

which is YOU.

Expressing your Talents.

Expressing your Skills.

Expressing your Abilities.

Expressing your Knowledge.

Expressing your Wisdom.

Expressing your Uniqueness.

Expressing your Divinity.

Expressing your True Natural Self.

And doing all of it through the lens...

Expressing all of it through the use of
God's Light and God's Love inside of you.

And having that refracted through the lens
of the Lighthouse of your Life.

You are God's greatest gift to the world.

You are God's Light that shines and brightens
the path for the people around you.

You are God's Love of a stranger when they need it.

You are God's Light and God's Love...
as I AM God's Light and God's Love.

I AM Oneness with God as you have
eternal Oneness with God.

The BOOK of LIGHT

"Let There Be" Divine Decrees

Let there be Light.

Let there be Love.

Let there be God's Masterpiece
Expressed in every Human Being.

Let there be God's Glory made
Manifest in every Moment.

Let there be God's Greatest Creation
expressed from your Divinity.

Let there be God's Greatest Creation expressed
throughout all of Humanity and all of Societies.

Let there be Great Joy Forevermore on Planet Earth.

Let there be Unity transforming All of Societies.

Let there be Cooperation that
Brings God's People Together.

The BOOK of LIGHT

Let there be Riches and Wealth
that have yet to be experienced here on Earth.

Let there be Heaven and the Highest Realms
of the Heavens Right Here and Now.

Let there be Great Love and Joy
from the Angels and the Archangels.

Let there be God's Love
as expressed through Jesus the Christ.

Let there be Light.

Let there be Love.

Let there be God's Love Beyond Measure.

Let there be the Immensity of God's Light within Me.

Let there be God's Love to the Depths of my Being.

Let there be God's Light

to the Furthest Expanse of Creation.

Let there be God made Manifest in Human Form.

Let there be Light.

Let there be Light.

And as the use of God's Light by you transforms every aspect of your being, your life as you know it will never be the same.

All aspects of your human Life will improve.

All aspects of your Eternal Life will

Magnify,

Amplify and

Expand.

All aspects of God's Light and God's Love within you, and around you, and in all aspects of the world that you live in, will be the permanent construct which has always been within you, which has never been separate from you.

You living in your Heart, you living in your Soul, you living in your Divinity, you living in your Christ Consciousness, you living in the Christ within you, you living with the knowing of God within you.

And making that as God has always intended for it to be the way you operate, and the way that you experience life as God always intended it to be...

Where You Experience Paradise.

You Experience Love.

You Experience Joy.

And You Experience Life in

Beautiful,

Wonderful,

Magnificent,

Happy and

Uplifting ways.

God Only Makes Perfect Things!

And as you live in the perfection of God's Light and Love within you, you will realize, you will experience, and you will know the perfection in your life and in the world around you, and in All of Creation.

I Love you Forevermore.

I Bless you with God's Light and God's Love.

I Bless you with that Now and Forever.

And I Love you with all the

Immensity of God's Love and Light within You.

I Love you so much.

I Love you so much.

Jesus the Christ

The BOOK of LIGHT

The BOOK of LIGHT

Chapter Six

The Light of God Always Wins

The Light of God Always Wins.

The Light of God Always Prevails.

The Light of God is Always Victorious.

It is only in your Consciousness, with the perception of living in a reality where there seems to be good and bad, good versus evil, God and the devil, and many other perceptions of polarizing energies.

But from the perspective of God, and the perspective of the Light of God within you, there is only well-being.

You are able to see through the illusion that once had you confused, that once had you scared and afraid, that once upon a time had you stressed out, worried and anxious.

But that ever expanding, ever more intense Light of God within you; from that point of truth within your Consciousness, the illusory reality that you live in does not have the same effect on you.

Because You Have Truly Overcome This World!

101

By living in the full expression of God's Light within you, with the full expression of God's Love within you, and from that place of knowing you are able to shine so much Light, and radiate so much Love that the things that once triggered your mind, the events of the world that once caused you to react in a state of fear, anxiety, sadness, depression, anger, hatred, rage; the experience of reality no longer has that effect on you.

When you have the permanent understanding and knowing of God's Light within you, and you flood your Mind, you flood your Body, you flood your entire Being, you flood Yourself, your Godself, you flood and saturate your entire Being, and all aspects of your Being, and all aspects of Yourself, with the Light of God.

You are Free!

There is Nothing in this World

that has the Power to affect

your Internal State of Being!

But once again, the conditioning of your consciousness by those around you and the environments that you grew up in, conditioned you to believe that you were small within a world that was big, that you were weak within a world where there were powers that were out to harm you.

You believed in these things because that's what you were taught, but from your eternal, everlasting perspective, which is the perspective of God within you, the perspective that you have while the Light of God shines through your Mind and through your Consciousness; with that perspective, those images, those events that happened in the world, those reports that you hear in the news, the stories that you hear from friends and relatives that are based on fear, or based on gossip...

Your Knowing is so Strong and Rooted in the Light of God

that you Truly have Divine Intelligence.

You are Truly Living in your Divine Intellect.

You can No Longer be Fooled.

You have God's Supreme Wisdom.

You can No Longer be Manipulated.

The BOOK of LIGHT

You see beyond the story and even the
supposed facts that are presented to you.

And you see beyond those details
and you perceive the truth;
you perceive lies,
you perceive manipulation
and it enables you to steer your path,
steer your ship in this ocean of life...

You steer Your Ship into Calm Waters.

And those calm waters are
the Peace,
the Love,
the Light
of God within you.

And as you are no longer reactive to what used to be a horrific or terrorizing story, you sit there in peaceful stillness, you see the illusion for what it is... just a series of images, moving pictures if you will, that you are viewing with your human eyes.

But now you are Perceiving

with the Perceptions that God has...

Perceiving Life from the Perception

of God's Light.

Perceiving Life from the Perception

of God's Love.

Watching the story unfold before your eyes knowing that you can give any meaning to any story, event or situation that you ever experience.

To see beyond the illusion, to see beyond the story that you experience with your physical senses, to see God's Light shining brightly from within, to see God's Love radiating from within every aspect of the scene that you are experiencing.

Just as an actor would be on the set experiencing life within a certain location and time.

You are just like that Actor.

You are the Main Character in your Life.

You are Experiencing the Set.

The only thing missing are the Cameras...

Lights, Camera, Action!

Then when you live in that knowing where you aren't reactive to the story, and you aren't reacting to the illusion, you send out such a high intensity frequency and vibration of energy.

You truly create what you imagine in your mind.

You can truly choose the reality

and the world that you live in.

Because you are projecting your thoughts and your emotions onto the screen of life, and then viewing life like that movie screen with a happy and pleasant smile on your face.

Because you know that you have created something that beautiful by aligning with your True self, aligning with your Godself, living in your Heart and Soul.

Living in God's Light and God's Love.

Beaming that from within Yourself

into the World around You.

Then Creating a Reality that is

Beautiful,

Magnificent,

Wonderful,

and Heavenly.

Right here,

right where you are at

in this Present Moment.

It is so exciting for me to share these words, concepts and ideas with you.

You truly are the creator of your life, and the co-creator of your life with God within you.

And as you access more of your purest Divinity, the purest form of your Consciousness, as you go deep within yourself to align with the Christ within you, the message that you send out from the Core of your Being through All of Creation is one that unifies with the Heavenly Realms, and unifies with the highest frequencies of the Heavenly Realms, and anchors that energy into your life and into the life for others on planet Earth.

It is Beautiful to see You and help You...

BE the Light of the World.

BE the Love of God in Human Form.

And as you radiate that Light and Love into the world around you, all that is unlike that Light and Love will dissolve, as you have the Power, Strength, and God Force within you to be the bright, shining Light and radiant example of God's magnificence in human form.

The BOOK of LIGHT

You are that Special.

You are that Wonderful.

You are that Brilliant.

You are that Magnificent.

You are that Spectacular.

You are that Splendid.

You are all of God's Greatness.

You are all of God's Light.

You are all of God's Love.

You are God in Action... as I AM God in Action.

God is Within You.

Every move you make, every thought you think, every emotion you feel, everything you experience; you experience along with the Creator of the Universe, who is experiencing all of it along with you.

So, as I close this chapter, know that the more that you embody God's Light and God's Love, the more that you align with God within you, the Creator of All that is, right there deep in your Consciousness, the more of a great experience that you and God are having together.

You are Always One with God.

You are Always Unified with God.

You have never been separated from God...

Although that is a perception

that you once believed.

The BOOK of LIGHT

You are God's Light.

You are God's Love.

You are God's Greatest Masterpiece.

God's Love for You Never Fails.

God's Light Always Wins.

God's Light is Everlasting and Always Victorious.

God's Light IS.

God's Love IS.

The BOOK of LIGHT

Blessings from Jesus

From my heart to your heart I Bless you with this message of God's Light intertwined with your permanent knowing and experience of God's Love within you as well.

God's Light Shines so Bright within You.

God's Love will Always uplift You.

God's Joy is Permanently in Every Beat of your Heart and

Pulses with Every Beat of your Heart.

God's Everlasting Well-Being is your Permanent State.

God Loves you Now and Forever...

as I Love you Now in Forever.

God's Light Shines in you Now and Forever,

as the Light of God in me

Shines in you Now and Forever.

Father, Son, and Holy Spirit...

We are One...

as You are One

with the Father,

with the Son,

and with the Holy Spirit.

You are Blessed and Glorified

as God's most Precious,

Loved and Adored Creation.

God Loves You...

As I Love You.

The BOOK of LIGHT

It is with Eternal Joyous Exultation

that I close this Book of Light,

and the message of God's Eternal Light within you!

God's Light Reigns Supreme!

The Light within you Always Wins!

The Love of God within You is Forevermore.

God's Infinite Blessings upon Your Life

Now and Forevermore.

I Love you. I Love you. I Love you.

Jesus the Christ

The BOOK of LIGHT

Final Words and Declarations
from Jesus the Christ

God's Light is in Everything,

Everywhere in All of Creation.

God spoke the Universe into existence

by saying "Let there be Light"

and with those words there was

Infinite Light everywhere.

There is no separation from God's Light.

God's Light is within You.

God's Light is within Me.

God's Light is within Everyone

and Everything, Everywhere.

Knowing that you carry God's

purest Light in your Divinity,

in the Core of your Being,

living in that Knowing is

living within a state of

Freedom.

The Freedom that you will experience...

By anchoring yourself into the
Light of God within you,

By anchoring your Mind and Body
into the Core of your Divinity,

By being completely One with the
Light and the Love of the Creator of All that is...

Life as you know it will never be the same,

as is always the case,

but from this state of Consciousness

your Life will improve and become...

The BOOK of LIGHT

More Beautiful.

More Magnificent.

More Radiant.

More Loving.

More Fun.

More Joyous.

More Fantastic.

More Glorious.

More Wonderful.

More Special.

More Spectacular.

More Prosperous. More Abundant.

And you will have the greatest sense of well-being throughout your entire Being that you have ever experienced before.

The Light of God within you, combined with the Love of God within you, is the intelligence of God, the radiant, loving energy of God that combine impeccably to create your life and the glorious reality that you will now experience.

Your Heaven on Earth is right there

in the Middle of your Consciousness.

You do not have to die, knowing again that death is just a perception within a human's consciousness, when you live with the eternal knowing in this present moment of God's Light and Love within you.

Heaven is Within You.

Heaven is Here and Now.

And as you deepen your knowing of this...

When you go into the depths of the
Light that God shines from within you...

When you expand to the
farthest reaches of All of Creation,
and you have the awareness
of that Light of God
that is ever expanding in your experience...

When you have that along with that deep,
immense Ocean of God's Love in you...

And the everlasting uplifting,
empowering Love of God expanding
throughout All of Creation around you...

You reinforce the knowing of the
Kingdom of God within you.

The Kingdom of God is Heaven.

Heaven is within You.

God's Light is within You.

God's Love is within You.

The BOOK of LIGHT

And as you once again remember what you already know;

to live with God's Light,

God's Love and

the Kingdom of Heaven,

and the Kingdom of God which is Heaven,

then you live with that in your Heart,

you live with that in your Soul,

you live with that in your Divinity,

you live with that in your Christ Consciousness,

you live with that in your Divine Blueprint,

you live with that in the depths of your Being,

as well as in your Spirit,

in your Mind,

in your Body,

in your True self,

in your Godself,

in your Higher self,

in all aspects that you Are...

The BOOK of LIGHT

You anchor Light, Love and Heaven

into this Glorious Present Moment

in the most Perfect

Here and Now...

And it is Forever Sustained,

Maintained,

Expanded upon,

Magnified and

Glorified!

The Eternal Present Moment

is an eternal present moment

to experience with the full expression of

God's Light and God's Love within you,

and the Kingdom of God

which is the Kingdom of Heaven within you,

right Here and right Now.

God Loves You Eternally, as I Love You Eternally.

You are Blessed Beyond Measure.

You are Blessed and Highly Favored.

You are God's Light that Shines within this World.

You are God's Love that

Uplifts the World around You.

You are the Presence of God,

and the Presence of God is within You.

Live in that Knowing.

Live in that State of Consciousness.

Live in that Awareness.

Live from that Eternal Perfection.

Your Divinity.

Your Purity.

God Loves You Now and Forevermore.

As I Love You Now and Forevermore.

The BOOK of LIGHT

The Light of God Never Fails.

The Light of God Always Wins.

The Light of God is Always Victorious.

As you are Always Victorious

as a bearer of God's Light,

within this Beautiful World

that you are experiencing.

Peace be with you Now and Forevermore.

I Love you and I Love you.

And with God's greatest, Loving embrace...

I leave you in that Eternal embrace.

The Eternal embrace of God's Love,

holding you for All of Eternity.

The BOOK of LIGHT

Divine Decrees of Light

I AM the Light of the World.

I AM the Light that Never Fails.

I AM the Light that Always Wins.

I AM God's Light that is Always Victorious.

I AM the Light that Brightens the Darkest of Corners.

I AM the Light of God's Purest Perfection.

I AM the Light Amplified by the
Angels and the Archangels.

I AM God's Light from the Beginning of Creation.

I AM God's Light Ever Increasing
in Brilliance and Splendor.

The BOOK of LIGHT

I AM Light which Transforms
All of my Thoughts into Thoughts of Perfection.

I AM Light that Transforms Every
Environment I spend time in.

I AM the Light that Shines in the
midst of the Darkness.

I AM the Light of God that Shines from the
Hearts and Minds of all of God's People.

I AM the Light that Radiates from the
Heart of Jesus Christ.

I AM the Light that is Always
Expanding and is Everlasting.

I AM God's Light in Human Form.

I AM God's Light, Eternal and Everlasting.

I AM God's Light,
Everlasting and Ever Blasting
for all of Infinity.

The BOOK of LIGHT

I AM the Light of God that Shines for all of Eternity.

I AM the Light of the World.

I AM the Light of God in the Smile of a Child.

I AM the Light that Transmutes any Disagreements.

I AM the Light that Transmutes
all forms of corruption.

I AM the Light that Glorifies God in the Highest.

I AM the Light that Radiates from the
Smile of God's Happy Servant.

I AM the Light of God which passes
all Human understanding.

I AM the Light of God Anchored
Deep within my Consciousness.

I AM the Light of God in all of my Endeavors.

The BOOK of LIGHT

I AM the Light of God in all of my Actions.

I AM the Light of God that
experiences only Perfection.

I AM the Light of God in all of my Perspectives.

I AM the Light of God in
Everything that my Eyes See.

I AM the Light of God in
Every Word that my Ears Hear.

I AM the Light of God within Everything
I Perceive with my Physical Senses.

I AM the Light of God that
Saturates my Entire Consciousness.

I AM the Light of the Creator within Me.

I AM the Light of the
Christ Consciousness within Me.

I AM the Light.

I AM God's Light.

I AM God's Everlasting, Purest,
most Beautiful, Radiant Light.

And it is Now... and it is Forevermore.

Amen.

And Amen.

And the Angels Sing!

Hallelujah and Amen!

About the Author

Daniel Prok is a God and Jesus loving
actor, writer, life coach and leader who is
creating Heaven on Earth.

He resides in La Jolla, California
and Sedona, Arizona.

For more content from Daniel to
improve your life go to...

www.DanielProk.com

Also, subscribe to Daniel Prok on Youtube.

And follow Daniel Prok on Facebook and Instagram.

Share the Message

The words in this book are so powerful that as you read, embody and live this message you will create a literal Heaven on Earth for yourself and for your LIFE.

And now is the time to Go Forth, as Jesus has said, and Share this message with the world as we create Heaven on Earth for the Collective.

Share these concepts with friends and loved ones.

Give books to your family and friends.

Give books as gifts for Christmas.

Supply books for your church, schools and organizations.

Be the Light that lights the path in the lives of those around you, as we experience this beautiful Planet Earth, the Garden of Eden, as is the Original Plan for our glorious home.

I Love you and I Bless you!

Daniel Prok

More Books from Daniel Prok

Get all the books in this series called

"The BOOKS of HEAVEN on EARTH":

"The BOOK of LOVE"

"The BOOK of LIGHT"

"The BOOK of HEAVEN"

"The BOOK of LIFE"

"El LIBRO del AMOR"

Get them now as Paperback or eBooks online
and from book stores everywhere.

Get the audiobooks on Audible, iTunes and more.

For Bulk purchase orders and speaking requests, contact
Daniel Prok through social media or email
danprokleader@gmail.com.

God Bless you with Love, Light, Heaven and Life!

Made in the USA
Las Vegas, NV
01 October 2021

31531681R00089